# Hearing What I Hear, Seeing What I See

## A Poetic Journey through PTSD

MEGHAN DILLEY

To order additional copies of this book, contact:
Xlibris
844-714-8691
www.Xlibris.com
Orders@Xlibris.com

ISBN:        Softcover              978-1-6641-8560-9
             EBook                 978-1-6641-8559-3

Print information available on the last page

Rev. date: 07/28/2021

# Acknowledgement

I would like to thank all those who have been part of my ever changing journey through PTSD. I am grateful for the support that I have received from family and friends old and new, my psychologist and psychiatrist. I hope you know who you are. Thank you to those who received an early glimpse into my work and reassured me to keep writing. Most importantly, I would like to thank Shanta Pamphile, MA, LPC, LMHC, NCC, ACS who has helped guide me through the toughest struggle of my life. She encouraged me and gave me the confidence to publish these poems. They are very personal and a very real depiction of my daily struggles and management of PTSD. I am very grateful to those who have understood me from the beginning, those who are starting to understand me, and those who do not or will never. This is me and my daily work in order to balance the wave.

# The Journey

Telling people how I feel
How everything still feels so real
Helps and then it doesn't
People I trust understand
But then they don't

How odd, I trust one I've known for four months
Over those I've known for 41 years
Who can't see me for anything besides what I was
Who say they understand, then feel I should be that girl
Who only sees the good and is always strong.

One day and a world of bumps have transformed me
As I try to dig out and do things to heal
I want to see the positives and do
But they are clouded by the grotesque images
From a beautiful sunny April day

And I can't forget!

# The Stranger

A stranger: calm, warm, and present
Knows more about me than myself
Engages me through tough sessions
To heal the trauma grappling within
I try not to look away.

Trauma that will remain, but dampened
Through talk, therapy, and relapse
Hands over ears in a quiet space, memories return
Relapse is welcomed
Showing healing is possible by understanding one's needs.

This new stranger has learned to welcome the other stranger
And has connected, realizing neither are strangers any longer
She is grateful with the internal self and physical presence
Who guided and continues to guide her
Through the toughest journey of her life.

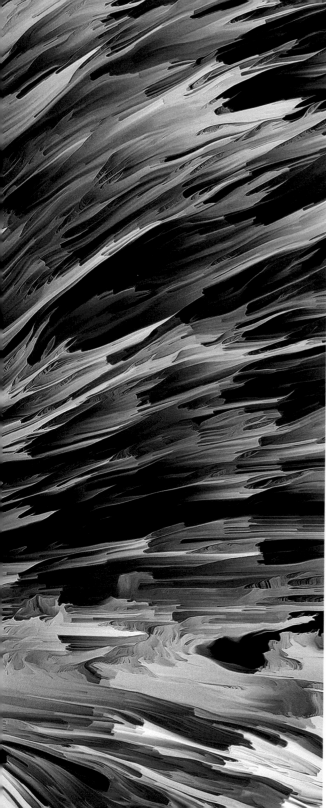

# Shelter

Protection from the world, from where does it come
A covering, a room, a cat, friends, from within
Why is it needed when it wasn't before
Not physically, but emotionally from feelings and symptoms stored
From noises that aren't threatening, but are
Because the memories attached invade.

Noises so subtle, but intense and unsettling
Motors, everyday sounds, so slight cause attention then inattention
a startling reaction kept mostly concealed
Soothed through those who know me and allow me to open up and heal
They have seen me at my most vulnerable and unprotected.
They let me be

My protection is gone and I am left with me.

# The Beautiful Symphony

It starts with a single noise so slight
A car zooms by
Few hear it
Then another with a single motor that sounds like a drone
Gets louder and louder
More noise chimes in a beautiful symphony
But not to some
It evokes fear, irritation
And the volume can't be turned down
There is no place of solace as you try to press on
It gets worse
It isolates because no one else hears it
But even in isolation it blares
Pounds in your head
You want to turn it off, slow it down, but can't
Until you find satisfying noises of peace in nature's path
A bird chirping, a brook calling
Which soothe you for at least the moment
With the beautiful symphony of lyrics from another time
Where do you find your beautiful symphony?

7

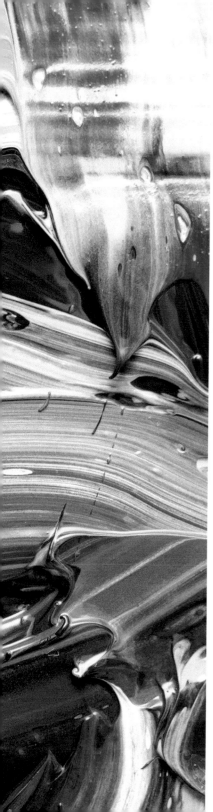

# The Mask

Locked away emotions, thoughts and words build
As your ears learn stories of others and are instilled
Those around you are loquacious as their words overpower
But yours although poetic lay hidden except on paper and cower

You listen and listen learning other's languages, cultures, and pains
But what is your story that you share muffled through a mask that remains?
Why do you stay silent with those who are closest?
Do their loudness and openness silence you from thoughts that lay deepest?

As your thoughts and words burrow deeper within, you don't speak,
Although your words yearn to escape, they continue to accumulate on paper and lay meek.
But on paper are they not real until spoken aloud
The emotions of others bombard you as yours are buried by a cloud.

Your accolades, pains, and speech are obscured.
Shrouded by the years past, but begin to seep toward
As through a filter, little by little and day by day
As your journey becomes clearer through your pains, your words stay

Sand accumulates grain by grain to form your story still hidden
But beginning to become unmasked from what was once forbidden.

# The Balance in A Wave

The crashing wave touches the sand and fades back into the sea
A thing of beauty that puts you at ease as you reflect on life's journey
The ebb and flow and you are at peace
The noise and strength of the waves can evoke melancholy, fear and anger
But not from the loud reverberations of the wave against a rock

A motor is heard in the distance, the heat ignites, an unknown clamor in the night
You jolt and are awake, 2:00 AM, in a refrigerator,
A memory, a constant, overwhelmed and enveloped by sensations in an enclosed fixture
That were suppressed at the time, a calm current erupts
A wave of emotions that are more welcomed, but not this noise

You look for the crashing tranquility of the wave
And its different elements that make you who you are
As it changes based on the currents and the eyes of the viewer
The currents of life that change and are not constant
Like the sound and reminders of the day

You are forever changed and changing like the wave
and at peace as the music of the sea soothes you and your fears
More welcomed as they lay intertwined in that wave that enters then returns to the sea.

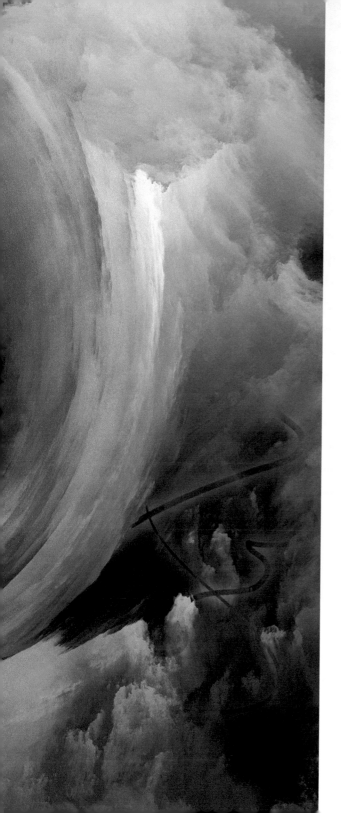

# The Scars Some Forget

She is coming over, I need to dress up
He is coming over I can wear sweats
Watching a game
Who am I?

A chameleon changing my skin based on who I'm around
But the same on the inside
Relating to so many
But who am I?

Tattoos, poems, sports, nature, a therapist
Hiding the tattoos and scars from those who don't understand
Under a long sleeve and mask
Do I pretend?

That day changed me, but made me who I am
Words begin to flow more easily about that day
As the words shed from the wounds
Healing continues, emotions spew.

But she doesn't remember the words
And they burrow back under the scars and tattoos
The words buried and disappear
Why doesn't she remember who I am?

# Finding the Aperture

Encapsulated in a world of sound
Made worse by some enclosures and better by others
An elevator with a motor brings you back
Your heart races

Your emotions are trapped
As they were in the refrigerator
Helping another with an unimagined task
The door closed

You kept your fears and emotions inside
Said it will be ok, bodies below you covered in bags
You stayed numb even as you swung the door open
You were free, so you thought

Back in the 70 degree sunny day
But 10 months later you are in an elevator
Covering your ears, the harsh sound of the motor
You see the faces of the bodies

You place an object in an oversized-garbage bag
You see the bodies
But the elevator is different
And your emotions can escape if you let them

Relief sets in as the doors release
A choice is to be made to keep thoughts buried
Or let them out

When you ride the elevator, more fear sets in
But you don't hide from it
You acknowledge it, although embarrassed at first
It doesn't stop you, but affects you

Does it affect you more when alone?
The realization is there,
vulnerable and unprotected, the doors open
Or when covered up to protect others
Used as a distraction from your fears, the doors close.

# The Hat

A ski hat sits atop your head as you gaze down the mountain
Protection from the cold and elements of nature
Various styles, shapes, materials and colors create the diverse landscape below
Keeping those outdoors safe

But what happens when this hat is required for another form of security
A different type of hat, not what it was intended for
Worn indoors to close out the artificial noise
That blares from the heat, the elevator motor, and people.

Unheard to most, noxious to you
But not heard when gliding down the snow slope.
The normalcy of wearing a hat in the cold
Questioned and judged when needed to protect from the inside elements that hurt you

A hat not needed in the snow, but worn due to its acceptance
But inside you are questioned, are you cold, are you sick?
In a space that overwhelms, it focuses you by quietly lowering the noise,
Just enough to allow you to do your work

If people only knew the protection from that hat
But you take it off and suffer because it is not accepted
It is not understood because its job is to protect you from the cold
What will protect you when ski hats are out of season and you are forced to remove it?

# The View

Driving through the town things look the same
The semblance of restaurants and businesses
Opened and reopened
Their facades look untouched
Cars zoom by, nothing has changed

But beyond these walls lay something very different
A mask continues to cover what is tarnished
Passing a local animal hospital you view a dog on a stretcher
The mask falls off
The view you see is something even more horrifying

The mask falls off again while hiking
More incredible views are seen
Sights that change every time you walk through the woods
It unveils deep beauty as you escape the mask

Sometimes the view below the mask is disturbing
The memories hurt and cause you to shutter
This is not what you intended to see

Other times it reveals a beautiful landscape
That constantly changes each time you walk the path.
This is not what you intended to see.

The town may look the same,
You may look the same,
The façade remains

But things are not the same, will never be the same
The mask is off and it is ok.

# The Double Meaning

You step inside, overwhelmed
You don't know why
No visible trigger brings you back to that day
You casually walk around
Seemingly protected by four walls
You pass the candy aisle of CVS and it worsens
You need to escape
Questioning why your hat doesn't protect you

The mild refrigeration hum of protection screams at you
It does not protect you – the hum gets louder
The trigger is understood
As you see a box that keeps objects from spoiling

The refrigerator from that day has a different meaning
It left things spoiled although its intention was to keep things alive
Perishables placed inside to keep them fresh
This box housed those perished
The door left open so spoiling of the bodies occurred
The door closed, the spoiling of me

My healing and transformation from the day is apparent
But the double meaning of a device used to preserve
Is also now understood
You hear the hum and you are locked inside
Searching for a purring cat or the soothing ocean waves
Healing continues as you are no longer locked inside.

# Sight

Leaving, thoughts run in circles
As you run through trails
They hear, but not what you hear
They see, but not what you see
One hears the noise, but doesn't understand
One doesn't hear the noise, so doesn't understand
Yet a three year old realizes the affect
Memories and symptoms made worse
By certain noises and loud noises
She tries to mute it
How can this be?
She alerts a seven year old friend not to make loud noises
Because of its affect on me
I can be understood
It can be done
By those of few years in this world
Is this why?
Others conditioned to see and hear but not listen
Or understand can come with age
This hurts
But there is hope
As a young child sees, not what you saw
Hears not what you heard
But understands how to make you feel better
Without being judged for what you are
Or what you hear.

# The Weight

Weight and resistance is added to your knee
It gains strength
With time
Initial pain occurs, swelling occurs
Although, not easy
Healing occurs, progress made, muscle strengthens
With time
Weight is added to your mind
A mind affected by trauma
You revert to the struggle, the triggers
With time
More weight is added, pressing down on you
You sink and can't escape
With time
It is reality
Added weight does not make you stronger
With time
You improve, but the weight lingers
Bringing you back
Carefully, you try to the balance the weight to float

Printed in the United States
by Baker & Taylor Publisher Services